Bolivia: A Guide to the Political History of Hispanic America's Poorest Nation

Copyright Page

TITLE: Bolivia: A Guide to the Political History of Hispanic America's Poorest Nation

1ST Edition

ISBN: 9798215371657

Bolivia: A Guide to the Political History of Hispanic America's Poorest Nation

By Roberto Miguel Rodriguez

Chapter 1: Bolivia: Political History of Hispanic America's Poorest Nation

Introduction to Bolivia's Political History

Bolivia: A Diplomat's Guide to Understanding the Political History of Hispanic America's Poorest Nation

As diplomats, it is crucial to have a comprehensive understanding of Bolivia's political history to effectively navigate the complex dynamics of this nation. Bolivia, known as Hispanic America's poorest nation, has a unique and fascinating political landscape shaped by various historical factors. This subchapter aims to provide an introduction to Bolivia's political history, highlighting key events, influential figures, and significant themes that have shaped the nation's trajectory.

Bolivia's role in the Latin American independence movement is a crucial starting point. The country played a pivotal role in the liberation of Latin America from Spanish colonial rule, with revolutionary leaders like Simón Bolívar and Antonio José de Sucre emerging from its soil. Understanding Bolivia's contribution to this movement provides valuable insights into the nation's struggle for autonomy and self-determination.

The impact of colonialism on Bolivia's political history cannot be overlooked. The Spanish colonization deeply influenced Bolivia's social, cultural, and political fabric, leaving a lasting imprint that continues to shape the nation today. The subjugation of indigenous peoples and the extraction of natural resources contributed to the marginalization and inequality that Bolivia grapples with to this day.

One of the most significant chapters in Bolivia's recent political history is the rise and fall of Evo Morales and the Movement for Socialism (MAS)

party. Morales, the first indigenous president of Bolivia, implemented progressive policies aimed at empowering marginalized communities. However, his prolonged presidency also witnessed controversies and challenges, leading to his eventual downfall. Understanding this era provides valuable insights into the complexities of Bolivia's political landscape.

The role of indigenous peoples in shaping Bolivia's political landscape is a central theme that cannot be ignored. Bolivia boasts a rich indigenous heritage, and the struggles and contributions of these communities have significantly influenced the nation's politics. Their demands for rights, recognition, and representation have played a pivotal role in shaping Bolivia's political dynamics.

Bolivia's struggles with political corruption and governance are critical aspects of its political history. The nation has faced persistent challenges in promoting transparent governance and combating corruption. Understanding these issues is essential for diplomats seeking to engage with Bolivia effectively.

The impact of natural resource extraction on Bolivia's political economy is another significant theme. Bolivia's rich natural resources, including gas, minerals, and lithium, have shaped its economic and political landscape. Understanding the complexities and challenges of managing these resources is crucial for diplomats engaging with Bolivia's political economy.

International organizations like the United Nations and World Bank have also played a role in Bolivia's political history. Their influence and involvement in shaping policies and providing assistance have had a profound impact on the nation's development trajectory.

The role of women in Bolivian politics and their fight for gender equality is an important aspect to consider. Women in Bolivia have been at the forefront of political movements, advocating for gender equality and leading transformative changes in society.

Bolivia's political relationship with its neighboring countries in South America is another crucial element to explore. The nation's regional dynamics and collaborations have influenced its politics and international relations.

Lastly, understanding the evolution of Bolivia's political parties and their ideologies throughout history provides valuable insights into the nation's shifting political landscape.

This subchapter serves as an introductory guide to Bolivia's political history, providing diplomats with a foundation to understand the complexities, challenges, and unique dynamics of this Hispanic American nation.

Pre-Colonial Era: Indigenous Political Systems

In the subchapter "Pre-Colonial Era: Indigenous Political Systems" of the book "Bolivia: A Diplomat's Guide to Understanding the Political History of Hispanic America's Poorest Nation," we delve into the rich and complex indigenous political systems that shaped Bolivia before colonization. This captivating era is crucial to understand Bolivia's political landscape today.

Indigenous peoples, such as the Quechua and Aymara, formed complex societies with well-defined political structures. These systems were characterized by decentralized governance, communal decision-making, and a close connection to the land. The central figure in these political systems was the community leader, often called a "mallku" or a "curaca," who held authority and made decisions in the best interest of the community.

These indigenous political systems were deeply rooted in egalitarianism and communal values. They fostered collective decision-making processes, where consensus and dialogue played a fundamental role. In addition, the indigenous peoples had a profound respect for nature and the environment, which influenced their political decisions and resource management strategies.

Understanding the pre-colonial era is crucial to comprehend Bolivia's political history, as it laid the foundation for the challenges and struggles faced by indigenous peoples throughout centuries of colonization and beyond. The subjugation and marginalization of indigenous communities by colonial powers profoundly impacted Bolivia's political landscape and social dynamics, leading to centuries of inequality and discrimination.

By studying the indigenous political systems, diplomats gain insights into the resilience and perseverance of Bolivia's indigenous peoples. These systems have played an instrumental role in shaping Bolivia's political landscape, as indigenous movements have fought for their rights, representation, and recognition. This subchapter provides a comprehensive understanding of the historical context that allowed the rise of indigenous political movements and their impact on Bolivia's political history.

In conclusion, the subchapter "Pre-Colonial Era: Indigenous Political Systems" explores the intricate and fascinating indigenous political systems that thrived in Bolivia before colonization. By understanding these systems, diplomats gain valuable insights into the resilience, cultural richness, and political struggles of Bolivia's indigenous peoples. This knowledge is crucial to contextualize Bolivia's political history and its ongoing challenges, such as the fight against inequality, corruption, and the quest for sustainable and inclusive governance.

Spanish Colonialism and its Impact on Bolivia

Spanish colonialism had a profound and lasting impact on Bolivia, shaping its political history and leaving a legacy that continues to influence the nation to this day. This subchapter aims to provide a comprehensive understanding of this historical period and its consequences, particularly for diplomats seeking to engage with Bolivia.

During the period of Spanish colonial rule, Bolivia, then known as Upper Peru, was a vital source of wealth for the Spanish Empire due to its rich deposits of silver and other natural resources. The exploitation of these resources led to the establishment of a rigid social hierarchy, with Spanish colonizers at the top and indigenous peoples at the bottom. This social division would have far-reaching implications for Bolivia's political landscape in the centuries to come.

Colonialism also introduced Catholicism as the dominant religion, which further reinforced the power of the Spanish elite and marginalized indigenous beliefs and practices. The Catholic Church became deeply intertwined with politics, exerting significant influence over Bolivian society and governance.

The impact of Spanish colonialism on Bolivia's political history is evident in the struggle for independence in the early 19th century. Bolivian leaders, inspired by the ideals of the French and American revolutions, fought for freedom from Spanish rule and the establishment of an independent nation. The legacy of colonialism, however, continued to shape the country's political institutions and social divisions long after independence was achieved.

One of the most significant consequences of Spanish colonialism was the marginalization of indigenous peoples. Despite constituting a majority of the population, indigenous communities faced discrimination and exclusion from political power for many years. This subchapter will explore the role of indigenous peoples in shaping Bolivia's political landscape, including their ongoing fight for recognition and representation.

The subchapter will also address Bolivia's struggles with political corruption and governance, which have plagued the country throughout its history. The extraction of natural resources, a legacy of colonialism, has often led to the exploitation of these resources by foreign companies, exacerbating economic inequality and political instability.

Additionally, the influence of international organizations like the United Nations and the World Bank on Bolivia's political history will be examined. These organizations have played a significant role in shaping Bolivia's economic policies and development strategies, often with mixed results.

Furthermore, the subchapter will discuss the role of women in Bolivian politics and their fight for gender equality. Despite facing significant barriers, women have made substantial strides in recent years, gaining greater representation and influence in political decision-making processes.

Lastly, the subchapter will explore Bolivia's political relationships with its neighboring countries in South America and the evolution of its political parties and their ideologies throughout history. This analysis will provide diplomats with a comprehensive understanding of Bolivia's regional dynamics and its political landscape.

In conclusion, Spanish colonialism had a profound and lasting impact on Bolivia. Understanding this historical period and its consequences is crucial for diplomats engaging with Bolivia, as it provides essential insights into the nation's political history, social divisions, struggles with corruption, and governance challenges.

Independence Movements in Hispanic America

The subchapter titled "Independence Movements in Hispanic America" delves into the crucial historical context that shaped Bolivia's political history and its role in the Latin American independence movement. This chapter aims to provide diplomats with a comprehensive understanding of the struggles, achievements, and complexities that influenced Bolivia's path to independence and subsequent political development.

Bolivia, one of Hispanic America's poorest nations, was deeply impacted by the colonial rule of the Spanish Empire. The legacy of colonialism left a lasting imprint on Bolivia's political landscape, with a social hierarchy that marginalized indigenous peoples and perpetuated inequality. The subchapter examines the origins of colonialism and its profound impact on Bolivia's political history, shedding light on the struggles faced by the country's diverse population.

Furthermore, the rise and fall of Evo Morales and the Movement for Socialism (MAS) party, a significant political force in Bolivia, are explored in detail. Diplomats will gain insights into the political ideology and socio-economic policies that shaped Bolivia during Morales' presidency, as well as the challenges faced by his government.

The subchapter also emphasizes the influential role played by indigenous peoples in shaping Bolivia's political landscape. It highlights their fight for recognition, representation, and the significant role they played in Bolivia's struggle for independence and in the subsequent formation of its political institutions.

Additionally, the content sheds light on Bolivia's struggles with political corruption and governance, which have hindered the country's development. Diplomats will gain an understanding of the challenges faced by Bolivia in creating transparent and accountable political systems.

The impact of natural resource extraction on Bolivia's political economy is also analyzed. The subchapter explores how Bolivia's rich natural resources, such as gas and minerals, have shaped its political economy and influenced the country's relationship with international organizations like the United Nations and the World Bank.

Furthermore, the subchapter discusses the role of women in Bolivian politics and their fight for gender equality. Diplomats will gain insights into the significant contributions made by women in Bolivia's political sphere and the challenges they continue to face in achieving equal representation.

Lastly, the subchapter explores Bolivia's political relationship with its neighboring countries in South America and the evolution of its political parties and their ideologies throughout history. Diplomats will gain a comprehensive overview of Bolivia's regional political dynamics and the ideologies that have shaped the country's political parties.

In conclusion, this subchapter provides diplomats with a deep understanding of the historical, social, and political intricacies that have defined Bolivia's political history. By examining its independence movements, colonial legacy, indigenous influence, struggles with corruption, and economic challenges, diplomats will be better equipped to navigate and engage with Bolivia's political landscape.

Bolivia's Role in the Latin American Independence Movement

The Latin American independence movement was a pivotal moment in the history of the region, and Bolivia played a significant role in this struggle for freedom and self-determination. This subchapter explores Bolivia's contribution to the movement, highlighting the key events and individuals that shaped the country's political history.

Bolivia, like other Latin American countries, was under Spanish colonial rule for centuries. However, the seeds of independence were sown in the late 18th century, with the ideas of the Enlightenment and the American and French Revolutions inspiring a new wave of political thinking. Bolivia's intellectual elite, including figures like Francisco de Miranda and Simón Bolívar, advocated for independence from Spanish rule and helped galvanize the movement across the continent.

One of the defining moments in Bolivia's quest for independence was the Battle of Ayacucho in 1824. Led by General Antonio José de Sucre, the Bolivian and allied forces achieved a decisive victory over the Spanish army, securing Bolivia's independence and marking a turning point in the Latin American independence movement.

However, Bolivia's road to political stability was far from smooth. The impact of colonialism on the country's political history cannot be understated. The legacy of Spanish rule left deep socioeconomic inequalities and a fragmented society, which hindered the formation of a strong, centralized government. This led to a series of political upheavals, coups, and dictatorships throughout Bolivia's history.

One figure who left an indelible mark on Bolivia's political landscape was Evo Morales and his Movement for Socialism (MAS) party. Morales, Bolivia's first indigenous president, came to power in 2006, promising to address the historical marginalization of indigenous peoples and combat poverty and inequality. Under his leadership, Bolivia experienced significant social and economic reforms, including the nationalization of natural resources and the redistribution of wealth.

However, Morales's presidency was not without controversy. Allegations of corruption and authoritarian tendencies marred his tenure, leading to widespread protests and ultimately his resignation in 2019. This event highlighted Bolivia's ongoing struggles with political corruption and governance.

Throughout Bolivia's history, indigenous peoples have played a crucial role in shaping the country's political landscape. Their fight for recognition and inclusion has been a driving force behind Bolivia's political evolution, leading to the enactment of progressive policies and the rise of indigenous leaders in recent years.

Moreover, Bolivia's political history has been influenced by international organizations such as the United Nations and the World Bank. These organizations have played a role in shaping Bolivia's development agenda and providing financial assistance for social and economic programs.

Women in Bolivia have also made significant strides in politics, fighting for gender equality and representation. Despite facing many challenges, women have been at the forefront of political movements and have made significant contributions to Bolivia's political landscape.

Furthermore, Bolivia's political relationship with its neighboring countries in South America has been a key factor in its history. The country has had both cooperative and contentious relationships with its neighbors, with issues such as territorial disputes and trade agreements shaping Bolivia's foreign policy.

Finally, the evolution of Bolivia's political parties and their ideologies throughout history has had a profound impact on the country's political landscape. From conservative and liberal parties in the early years of independence to the emergence of socialist and indigenous-led movements in recent decades, Bolivia's political parties reflect the ever-changing dynamics of the nation.

In conclusion, Bolivia's role in the Latin American independence movement cannot be overstated. From its fight for independence to its struggles with political corruption and governance, Bolivia's political history is a testament to the resilience and determination of its people.

Understanding Bolivia's past is crucial for diplomats and anyone interested in the intricate dynamics of Latin American politics.

Post-Independence Turmoil: Early Political Instability in Bolivia

Bolivia: A Diplomat's Guide to Understanding the Political History of Hispanic America's Poorest Nation delves into the complexities of Bolivia's political landscape. In this subchapter, we examine the post-independence turmoil and early political instability that shaped the nation.

Following its liberation from Spanish colonial rule in 1825, Bolivia faced a period of profound political instability. The struggle for power among competing factions led to a series of coups, uprisings, and short-lived governments. This volatility hindered the nation's ability to establish stable governance and impeded its socio-economic development.

The impact of colonialism on Bolivia's political history cannot be overlooked. The legacy of Spanish rule left deep divisions within society, perpetuating a cycle of political unrest. The dominant criollo elite, descended from Spanish conquerors, sought to maintain their privileged position, while indigenous groups fought for recognition and inclusion in the political sphere.

Bolivia's role in the Latin American independence movement also contributed to its early political turmoil. The country's geographical and ethnic diversity made it a fertile ground for competing ideologies and power struggles. This diversity, coupled with economic disparities and regional rivalries, further complicated the nation's political landscape.

The subchapter also explores the rise and fall of Evo Morales and the Movement for Socialism (MAS) party in Bolivia. Morales, the country's first indigenous president, initially brought hope for political stability and social justice. However, his prolonged stay in power, allegations of corruption, and attempts to consolidate power eroded public trust and led to widespread protests, culminating in his resignation in 2019.

Additionally, the role of indigenous peoples in shaping Bolivia's political landscape is examined. Their demands for recognition and representation have played a significant role in shaping the nation's political discourse, fostering a more inclusive democracy.

Furthermore, the subchapter delves into Bolivia's struggles with political corruption and governance. The country has long grappled with issues of transparency, accountability, and effective governance, which have hindered its development and perpetuated social inequality.

The impact of natural resource extraction on Bolivia's political economy is also explored. Bolivia's rich deposits of minerals and natural gas have attracted foreign investment, but their exploitation has often perpetuated economic dependence and exacerbated social and environmental challenges.

The subchapter also highlights the influence of international organizations like the United Nations and World Bank on Bolivia's political history. These entities have played a role in shaping Bolivia's development policies and providing assistance in areas such as poverty reduction and sustainable development.

The role of women in Bolivian politics and their fight for gender equality is another crucial aspect examined in this subchapter. Despite facing numerous challenges, women have made significant strides in recent years, working to achieve greater representation and influence in the political arena.

Lastly, Bolivia's political relationship with its neighboring countries in South America is explored, as well as the evolution of its political parties and their ideologies throughout history. Understanding these dynamics is crucial for diplomats seeking to navigate Bolivia's complex political landscape and foster positive relations with the nation.

In conclusion, the subchapter on post-independence turmoil and early political instability in Bolivia sheds light on the challenges faced by the nation in its quest for political stability, inclusive governance, and socio-economic development. Diplomats and those interested in Bolivia's political history will gain valuable insights into the factors that have shaped the nation's political landscape and continue to influence its future trajectory.

Chapter 2: The Impact of Colonialism on Bolivia's Political History

The Encomienda System and Subjugation of Indigenous Peoples

Chapter Summary: This subchapter delves into the Encomienda System and its profound impact on the subjugation of indigenous peoples in Bolivia. It explores the historical context, the consequences of this system, and its lasting effects on Bolivia's political history.

Content:

The Encomienda System was a colonial institution established by the Spanish conquistadors in the Americas during the 16th century. Under this system, indigenous peoples were forcefully assigned to Spanish settlers as laborers, effectively turning them into a form of serfdom. This subjugation of indigenous populations had a profound impact on Bolivia's political history.

The arrival of the Spanish conquistadors in Bolivia marked the beginning of the systematic exploitation and subjugation of indigenous peoples. The Encomienda System allowed the Spanish settlers to exploit the labor of indigenous communities, leading to the depletion of their resources and the destruction of their social structures.

The consequences of the Encomienda System were devastating for the indigenous peoples of Bolivia. Forced labor, harsh treatment, and diseases brought by the Spanish resulted in a significant decline in the indigenous population. Moreover, their cultures, languages, and traditions were suppressed, leading to a loss of identity and social cohesion.

The lasting effects of the Encomienda System can still be seen in Bolivia's political landscape today. Indigenous communities continue to face marginalization, discrimination, and limited access to political power. The historical trauma and the loss of cultural heritage have created lasting divisions within Bolivian society.

Understanding the Encomienda System is crucial for diplomats seeking to comprehend Bolivia's political history. It serves as a foundation for comprehending the struggles faced by indigenous communities and the ongoing fight for social justice and equality. Diplomats must recognize the importance of addressing historical injustices and promoting policies that empower and uplift indigenous peoples.

In conclusion, the Encomienda System was a key factor in the subjugation of indigenous peoples in Bolivia. Its legacy continues to shape Bolivia's political history, impacting the role of indigenous communities in shaping political landscapes and the ongoing fight for social justice. Diplomats must be aware of these historical dynamics to effectively engage with Bolivia's political realities and work towards a more inclusive and equitable society.

Social Hierarchies and the Legacy of Colonialism

The subchapter "Social Hierarchies and the Legacy of Colonialism" delves into the profound impact that centuries of colonial rule have had on Bolivia's political landscape and societal structure. This section aims to provide diplomats with a comprehensive understanding of the historical context that has shaped the country's complex power dynamics and social hierarchies.

Bolivia, as one of the poorest nations in Hispanic America, has a long and turbulent history of colonial exploitation. For centuries, the indigenous population was subjugated and marginalized by the Spanish colonizers, who imposed a rigid social hierarchy based on race and ethnicity. This legacy of colonialism is deeply entrenched in Bolivia's political history, influencing power structures and exacerbating socioeconomic inequalities.

The impact of colonialism on Bolivia's political history is undeniable. The Spanish colonizers systematically exploited Bolivia's vast natural resources, such as silver and tin, leading to the enrichment of a select few while leaving the majority of the population impoverished. This history of resource extraction has had lasting effects on Bolivia's political economy, perpetuating a cycle of dependence and inequality.

The rise and fall of Evo Morales and the Movement for Socialism (MAS) party is a testament to the complex interplay between social hierarchies and political power. Morales, Bolivia's first indigenous president, sought to challenge the entrenched social hierarchies by championing the rights of marginalized groups. His administration implemented policies aimed at empowering indigenous peoples and redistributing wealth, but it also faced significant opposition from entrenched elites.

The role of indigenous peoples in shaping Bolivia's political landscape cannot be overstated. Their resilience and resistance have been instrumental in challenging the status quo and pushing for greater inclusion and representation. However, Bolivia continues to struggle with political corruption and governance issues, hindering progress towards a more equitable society.

International organizations such as the United Nations and World Bank have played a significant role in Bolivia's political history, both positively and negatively. While they have provided support and funding for development initiatives, their influence has sometimes perpetuated the same neocolonial dynamics that have plagued the country for centuries.

Furthermore, the subchapter explores the fight for gender equality and the role of women in Bolivian politics. Despite significant challenges, women have been at the forefront of advocating for their rights and making strides towards a more inclusive political system.

Lastly, Bolivia's political relationship with its neighboring countries in South America and the evolution of its political parties and ideologies throughout history are examined. These aspects shed light on the external factors that have influenced Bolivia's political trajectory and continue to shape its regional dynamics.

In conclusion, the subchapter "Social Hierarchies and the Legacy of Colonialism" provides diplomats with a comprehensive understanding of the historical context that has shaped Bolivia's political history. By examining the impact of colonialism, social hierarchies, and the struggles for equality, diplomats can gain valuable insights into Bolivia's complex political landscape and contribute to more informed and effective diplomatic engagements.

Land Distribution and Land Reform

Land distribution and land reform have played a significant role in shaping Bolivia's political history. Understanding the complexities of this issue is crucial for diplomats seeking to comprehend the challenges faced by the country and its people.

Bolivia's land distribution has long been characterized by inequality and concentration of ownership. During the colonial era, vast stretches of land were controlled by a small elite, predominantly of European descent. This pattern continued even after Bolivia gained independence from Spain in the early 19th century, perpetuating social and economic disparities.

Land reform emerged as a central issue in Bolivia's political landscape during the 20th century. Various governments attempted to address the problem, but progress was slow and often hindered by powerful interest groups. The National Revolution of 1952 marked a turning point, as the government implemented significant agrarian reforms, aiming to redistribute land to indigenous communities and small farmers. These reforms, however, faced resistance from wealthy landowners and foreign companies with vested interests in Bolivia's natural resources.

The rise and fall of Evo Morales and the Movement for Socialism (MAS) party brought renewed attention to land reform in Bolivia. Morales, Bolivia's first indigenous president, championed the rights of indigenous peoples and pushed for greater land redistribution. Under his leadership, significant strides were made, particularly in favor of indigenous communities. However, tensions arose with sectors of the population that felt marginalized by these policies and saw their own land rights threatened.

Today, Bolivia continues to grapple with the challenges of land distribution and reform. The country's natural resource extraction, including mining and gas industries, further complicate the issue. While these industries bring economic benefits, they also contribute to environmental degradation and exacerbate social inequalities, particularly in rural areas.

International organizations, such as the United Nations and World Bank, have played a role in Bolivia's land reform efforts, providing support and guidance. Their involvement has been crucial in fostering dialogue between different stakeholders and promoting sustainable practices.

Bolivia's political parties have also evolved in their approaches to land distribution. Some advocate for the continuation of Morales' policies, while others propose alternative strategies that balance economic development with social justice and environmental sustainability.

In conclusion, land distribution and reform remain central issues in Bolivia's political history. Diplomats must understand the complexities and nuances of this topic to effectively engage with the country and contribute to its development. By promoting inclusive and sustainable land policies, Bolivia can address historical injustices, reduce inequality, and pave the way for a more prosperous future.

Indigenous Rights Movements and their Influence on Bolivian Politics

The indigenous rights movements have played a significant role in shaping Bolivia's political landscape and have had a profound influence on the country's politics. This subchapter aims to explore the various indigenous rights movements in Bolivia and their impact on the nation's political history.

Bolivia is home to a diverse range of indigenous communities, each with their distinct cultures, languages, and traditions. For centuries, these indigenous peoples have faced discrimination, marginalization, and the loss of their ancestral lands. However, in recent decades, they have organized themselves into powerful social and political movements to demand recognition, rights, and representation.

One of the most influential indigenous rights movements in Bolivia is the Confederation of Indigenous Peoples of Bolivia (CIDOB). Founded in 1982, CIDOB has been at the forefront of advocating for indigenous rights and has successfully pushed for constitutional reforms that recognize the rights of indigenous peoples, including the right to self-determination, land rights, and cultural preservation.

Another prominent indigenous rights movement is the National Council of Ayllus and Markas of Qullasuyu (CONAMAQ). CONAMAQ represents indigenous communities in the highlands and has been instrumental in promoting indigenous autonomy and self-governance.

These movements have not only fought for indigenous rights but have also transformed Bolivia's political landscape. Their demands for greater representation and inclusion have led to the rise of indigenous leaders in politics. Evo Morales, an indigenous Aymara, became the first indigenous president of Bolivia in 2006, representing the Movement for Socialism (MAS) party.

The rise of Morales and MAS marked a significant shift in Bolivia's political history. Under Morales' leadership, Bolivia witnessed a series of progressive reforms aimed at empowering indigenous communities and addressing historical inequalities. These reforms included the nationalization of natural resources, land redistribution, and the promotion of indigenous languages and cultures.

However, Morales' presidency also faced challenges, including allegations of corruption and a controversial bid for a fourth term in office. This eventually led to his resignation in 2019 and a period of political instability in Bolivia.

Despite the challenges faced by indigenous rights movements, their influence on Bolivian politics remains significant. They continue to advocate for the rights of indigenous peoples, environmental protection, and social justice. The recognition and inclusion of indigenous perspectives in Bolivia's political landscape have become crucial for the country's development and democratic consolidation.

As diplomats, it is crucial to understand the role of indigenous rights movements in Bolivia's political history. Their demands and struggles shape the nation's policies, governance, and social dynamics. By engaging with these movements and supporting their causes, diplomats can contribute to fostering a more inclusive and equitable political environment in Bolivia.

Chapter 3: The Rise and Fall of Evo Morales and the Movement for Socialism (MAS) party in Bolivia

Evo Morales: Background and Early Political Career

Evo Morales, a prominent figure in Bolivia's political history, rose to power as the country's first indigenous president. Born on October 26, 1959, in the small rural community of Isallawi in Orinoca, Morales grew up in a humble Aymara indigenous family. His experiences as a farmer and herder shaped his deep understanding of the struggles faced by Bolivia's impoverished population.

Morales began his political career as a union leader, representing the coca farmers in the Chapare region. His advocacy for the rights of the indigenous population and his stance against U.S.-led efforts to eradicate coca cultivation propelled him into the national spotlight. Morales emerged as a charismatic leader, known for his ability to mobilize and unite various social movements.

In 1995, Morales founded the political party, the Movement for Socialism (MAS), with the aim of representing the marginalized sectors of Bolivian society. The party gained momentum and support, particularly from indigenous communities, due to its focus on social justice and economic redistribution.

Bolivia's history of colonialism had a profound impact on its political landscape, and Morales recognized the need to address the systemic inequalities that persisted. He aimed to challenge the traditional power structures and create a more inclusive political system that gave voice to the historically marginalized indigenous peoples.

Morales' rise to power came in 2005 when he won the presidential election with overwhelming support from Bolivia's indigenous population. His presidency marked a turning point in Bolivia's political history, as it symbolized the empowerment of indigenous peoples and the beginning of a new era of social transformation.

Throughout his time in office, Morales implemented various progressive policies aimed at reducing poverty, promoting social welfare, and nationalizing key industries. His government focused on the equitable distribution of wealth, using revenue from natural resource extraction to fund social programs and infrastructure development.

However, Morales faced numerous challenges during his presidency, including allegations of corruption and accusations of authoritarian tendencies. These controversies ultimately led to his resignation in 2019, following widespread protests and allegations of electoral fraud.

Despite the controversies surrounding Morales and his party, the MAS continues to be a significant force in Bolivian politics. The party's ideology, centered on indigenous rights and social justice, resonates with a significant portion of the population.

In conclusion, Evo Morales' background as an indigenous farmer and his early political career as a union leader laid the foundation for his transformative presidency. His rise to power represented a significant shift in Bolivia's political landscape, highlighting the role of indigenous peoples in shaping the country's history. Morales' time in office was marked by progressive policies aimed at addressing systemic inequalities, though his presidency was not without controversy. Nonetheless, his impact on Bolivia's political history cannot be overlooked, as it continues to shape the country's political landscape today.

The Rise of the MAS Party

Title: The Rise of the MAS Party: Bolivia's Political Transformation

Introduction:

In the tumultuous political landscape of Bolivia, few movements have had such a profound impact as the rise of the Movement for Socialism (MAS) party. This subchapter delves into the ascent of the MAS party, its charismatic leader Evo Morales, and the transformative effect they had on Bolivia's political history and society. By analyzing the factors that led to their rise, we gain a deeper understanding of Bolivia's complex political dynamics and its role in shaping the history of Hispanic America's poorest nation.

The Origins of the MAS Party:

The MAS party emerged in the early 1990s as a response to Bolivia's deep-rooted social and economic inequalities. With a strong focus on indigenous rights and social justice, the party quickly gained popularity among marginalized populations. The party's inclusive message, coupled with its charismatic leader Evo Morales, resonated with a broad spectrum of Bolivian society, particularly the indigenous communities.

The Rise to Power:

In 2005, Evo Morales made history by becoming Bolivia's first indigenous president, marking a significant turning point in the country's political landscape. Under his leadership, the MAS party implemented a series of progressive policies aimed at reducing poverty, empowering indigenous communities, and challenging the status quo. Morales' government implemented land reforms, nationalized key industries, and used revenue from natural resource extraction to fund social programs and infrastructure development.

Challenges and Achievements:

Despite its initial popularity, the MAS party faced significant challenges during its tenure. Allegations of corruption and a polarized political environment put a strain on Morales' presidency. However, the party's achievements in reducing poverty, improving access to education and healthcare, and advancing indigenous rights cannot be understated. The MAS party's policies played a crucial role in transforming Bolivia's political economy and empowering historically marginalized groups.

Legacy and Lessons Learned:

The rise and fall of the MAS party in Bolivia offers valuable insights into the complexities of political power and governance. It highlights the importance of inclusive policies, the role of indigenous peoples in shaping Bolivia's political landscape, and the challenges of managing natural resource extraction. Understanding the rise of the MAS party is essential for diplomats seeking to navigate Bolivia's intricate political history and engage with its diverse society.

Conclusion:

The rise of the MAS party in Bolivia marks a pivotal moment in the country's political history. Through an inclusive and progressive agenda, the party challenged traditional power structures and prioritized the needs of marginalized communities. While facing numerous challenges and criticism, the MAS party's legacy continues to shape Bolivia's political landscape. By recognizing and understanding the rise of the MAS party, diplomats can better comprehend Bolivia's complex history and contribute to the country's ongoing development and political transformation.

Morales' Presidency and the Implementation of Socialistic Policies

The presidency of Evo Morales and the implementation of socialistic policies marked a significant turning point in Bolivia's political history. Morales, a member of the indigenous Aymara community, became the country's first indigenous president in 2006, promising to address the deep-rooted inequalities that have plagued Bolivia for centuries.

Under Morales' leadership, the Movement for Socialism (MAS) party sought to tackle poverty, social exclusion, and the marginalization of indigenous communities. Morales believed that the state should play a central role in the economy to ensure wealth redistribution and promote social justice.

One of the key initiatives of Morales' presidency was the nationalization of natural resources, particularly the gas and oil industries. This move aimed to regain control over Bolivia's rich natural resources and ensure that they were used to benefit the Bolivian people. Morales argued that previous governments had allowed foreign companies to exploit Bolivia's resources without adequately benefiting the local population.

Another significant policy implemented during Morales' presidency was the redistribution of land. Bolivia has long struggled with land inequality, with a small elite owning the majority of fertile land while the majority of peasants and indigenous communities had limited access to land for agriculture. Morales aimed to address this issue by implementing land reforms that redistributed land to landless farmers and indigenous communities.

Furthermore, Morales' administration focused on social programs and welfare policies to reduce poverty and improve access to education, healthcare, and social services. These efforts included the implementation of cash transfer programs, the expansion of healthcare facilities in rural areas, and the provision of free education.

However, Morales' presidency was not without controversy. Critics argued that his government's socialistic policies were detrimental to the economy, stifled private investment, and led to increased government control over key sectors. Additionally, allegations of corruption and authoritarian tendencies overshadowed his tenure.

In conclusion, Morales' presidency and the implementation of socialistic policies represented a significant chapter in Bolivia's political history. While his government made strides in addressing social inequalities and empowering indigenous communities, it also faced challenges and criticism. Understanding Morales' presidency and the impact of socialistic policies is crucial for diplomats seeking to navigate Bolivia's political landscape and comprehend the country's socio-economic complexities.

Challenges and Controversies During Morales' Tenure

Evo Morales, a prominent figure in Bolivia's political history, served as the President of Bolivia from 2006 to 2019, making him the country's longest-serving leader. Morales, a member of the Movement for Socialism (MAS) party, came into power with a promise to bring about significant changes and improve the lives of the marginalized and indigenous populations in Bolivia. However, his tenure was not without its fair share of challenges and controversies.

One of the main challenges faced by Morales during his time in office was the struggle with political corruption and governance. Despite his efforts to combat corruption, allegations of nepotism and favoritism within his government persisted, casting doubt on his commitment to transparency and accountability. This challenged his credibility and led to growing discontent among the population.

Another controversy during Morales' tenure was the impact of natural resource extraction on Bolivia's political economy. Morales, initially hailed as a champion of indigenous rights and environmental conservation, faced criticism for his government's policies that prioritized economic growth over environmental sustainability. The extraction of natural resources, such as gas and minerals, led to conflicts with local communities and indigenous groups who felt their rights were being disregarded.

Furthermore, Morales' close relationship with international organizations like the United Nations and World Bank raised concerns about the influence of external actors on Bolivia's political history. Some critics argued that Morales was compromising Bolivia's sovereignty by aligning too closely with these organizations and adopting their policies, which often prioritized neoliberal economic reforms.

Gender equality was another contentious issue during Morales' tenure. While Morales emphasized the importance of women in Bolivian politics, there were ongoing struggles for gender equality. Despite implementing measures to increase women's representation, such as a gender quota in the legislature, progress was slow, and women continued to face barriers and discrimination in the political sphere.

Additionally, Morales' foreign policy and Bolivia's political relationship with its neighboring countries in South America also faced scrutiny. While he sought to strengthen regional integration and foster alliances with left-leaning governments in the region, his confrontational approach with some neighboring countries, such as Chile, led to tensions and strained diplomatic relations.

In conclusion, Evo Morales' tenure as President of Bolivia was marked by various challenges and controversies. From struggles with political corruption and governance to debates surrounding natural resource extraction and international influence, Morales faced significant obstacles in his pursuit of improving Bolivia's political landscape. These challenges and controversies shaped Bolivia's political history during Morales' tenure and continue to influence the country's political dynamics today.

The Fall of Morales and the Transition of Power

In the intricate tapestry of Bolivia's political history, few events have been as significant as the fall of Evo Morales and the subsequent transition of power. This chapter delves into the captivating saga of Morales' rise and fall, shedding light on the complex dynamics that shaped Bolivia's political landscape.

Evo Morales, a charismatic indigenous leader, became the first indigenous president of Bolivia in 2006. Riding on a wave of popular support, Morales and his party, the Movement for Socialism (MAS), promised to empower the marginalized indigenous population and combat the deep-rooted inequality that plagued the nation.

Under Morales' leadership, Bolivia experienced a period of economic growth and social progress. His policies, aimed at nationalizing natural resources and redistributing wealth, endeared him to many Bolivians. However, Morales' long tenure in power also led to accusations of authoritarianism and an erosion of democratic institutions.

The fall of Morales was triggered by widespread protests in 2019, following allegations of electoral fraud during the presidential elections. Diplomats closely observed the unfolding events, as Bolivia teetered on the brink of a political crisis. With mounting pressure from the military and international organizations, Morales resigned and fled the country, leaving a power vacuum in his wake.

The subsequent transition of power proved to be a delicate process, with interim governments struggling to restore stability and legitimacy. Diplomats played a crucial role in facilitating dialogue and mediating between different factions, as Bolivia grappled with the challenge of finding a new leader who could unite the deeply divided nation.

This subchapter also explores the role of international organizations, such as the United Nations and the World Bank, in Bolivia's political history. These organizations have exerted influence over Bolivia's economic policies and governance, shaping the country's trajectory and fostering both opportunities and challenges.

Furthermore, the subchapter highlights the resilience and determination of Bolivian women in fighting for gender equality and having a voice in politics. It also delves into Bolivia's complex relationships with its neighboring countries in South America, examining the dynamics of cooperation and tension that have shaped the region's political landscape.

By examining the fall of Morales and the subsequent transition of power, diplomats gain a deeper understanding of the intricate political history of Bolivia. This knowledge equips them to navigate the complexities of Bolivia's political landscape, fostering diplomatic relationships and promoting stability in the nation and the region at large.

Chapter 4: The Role of Indigenous Peoples in Shaping Bolivia's Political Landscape

Indigenous Movements and Activism in Bolivia

Bolivia, a nation with a rich cultural heritage, has witnessed a significant role played by indigenous movements and activism in shaping its political landscape. This subchapter delves into the profound influence of indigenous peoples on Bolivia's political history, their struggles, achievements, and the challenges they continue to face.

From the earliest days of colonization, indigenous communities in Bolivia have endured the brunt of oppression and marginalization. However, their resilience and determination to reclaim their rights have led to the emergence of powerful indigenous movements. These movements have spearheaded transformative political changes and paved the way for greater inclusion and representation.

One of the most notable indigenous movements in Bolivia's history is the rise of Evo Morales and the Movement for Socialism (MAS) party. Morales, an Aymara indigenous leader, became the country's first indigenous president in 2006, marking a significant milestone for indigenous peoples in Bolivia. Under his leadership, Bolivia witnessed unprecedented advancements in indigenous rights, land redistribution, and social justice reforms.

However, the story of indigenous movements in Bolivia goes beyond Morales and MAS. It is a story of resilience and collective action. Indigenous communities have fought for their land rights, cultural preservation, and recognition of their ancestral knowledge. They have organized protests, blockades, and mobilizations to demand justice and equality.

Despite the progress made, Bolivia continues to grapple with political corruption and governance challenges. Indigenous activists have been at the forefront of demanding transparency and accountability from the government. Their activism has been instrumental in exposing corruption scandals and pushing for institutional reforms.

Moreover, the impact of natural resource extraction on Bolivia's political economy cannot be understated. Indigenous communities residing in resource-rich areas have often borne the environmental and social costs of extraction. They have mobilized against the exploitation of their lands and resources, advocating for sustainable development and community empowerment.

International organizations like the United Nations and World Bank have also played a significant role in Bolivia's political history. Indigenous activists have leveraged these platforms to amplify their voices and advocate for their rights on the global stage. These organizations have provided support and resources to indigenous movements, enabling them to strengthen their political influence.

Furthermore, the subchapter explores the role of women in Bolivian politics and their ongoing fight for gender equality. Women have been at the forefront of indigenous movements, challenging traditional gender norms and demanding equal representation in decision-making processes.

Lastly, the subchapter sheds light on Bolivia's political relationship with its neighboring countries in South America and the evolution of its political parties and ideologies throughout history. It provides a comprehensive understanding of the dynamics that have shaped Bolivia's political landscape.

In conclusion, indigenous movements and activism have played a pivotal role in Bolivia's political history. From challenging colonialism to demanding social justice and indigenous rights, these movements have transformed the nation's political landscape. The struggle for equality and representation continues, and diplomats must recognize and engage with indigenous communities to foster an inclusive and prosperous Bolivia.

The Struggle for Indigenous Rights and Recognition

In the subchapter titled "The Struggle for Indigenous Rights and Recognition," we delve into the profound impact of indigenous peoples on shaping Bolivia's political landscape. This chapter aims to provide diplomats with a comprehensive understanding of the struggles faced by indigenous communities and their fight for recognition and rights.

Bolivia, as the poorest nation in Hispanic America, has a long history of marginalization and discrimination against its indigenous population. The legacy of colonialism has deeply influenced Bolivia's political history, perpetuating inequality and social exclusion. However, in recent decades, indigenous voices have gained momentum, demanding their rights and challenging the traditional power structures.

The rise and fall of Evo Morales and the Movement for Socialism (MAS) party in Bolivia exemplify the increased influence of indigenous peoples in politics. Morales, Bolivia's first indigenous president, brought significant changes to the country, prioritizing the rights and welfare of indigenous communities. His presidency marked a turning point in Bolivia's political history, as it witnessed the empowerment and inclusion of indigenous groups in decision-making processes.

Nevertheless, Bolivia's struggle for indigenous rights and recognition is far from over. The country continues to face challenges in combating political corruption and improving governance, which hinders the progress of indigenous communities. Additionally, the impact of natural resource extraction on Bolivia's political economy has further exacerbated inequalities and marginalized indigenous groups.

International organizations like the United Nations and the World Bank have played a crucial role in Bolivia's political history. Their involvement has provided support for indigenous rights and helped promote inclusive governance. However, more efforts are needed to address the complex issues faced by indigenous communities fully.

The subchapter also explores the role of women in Bolivian politics and their fight for gender equality. Women have played a significant role in shaping Bolivia's political landscape, advocating for their rights and challenging traditional gender norms.

Furthermore, Bolivia's political relationship with neighboring countries in South America is examined, as it influences the country's diplomatic strategies and regional alliances.

Lastly, the evolution of Bolivia's political parties and their ideologies throughout history is analyzed, highlighting the changing dynamics of political power and the varying perspectives on indigenous rights.

Overall, "The Struggle for Indigenous Rights and Recognition" provides diplomats with a comprehensive understanding of the challenges faced by indigenous communities in Bolivia and the ongoing fight for their rights and recognition. It emphasizes the importance of inclusive governance, social equality, and the empowerment of marginalized groups for Bolivia's future development.

Indigenous Representation in Bolivian Politics

Throughout its history, Bolivia has been shaped by the influence and participation of indigenous peoples in its political landscape. The subchapter on "Indigenous Representation in Bolivian Politics" examines the pivotal role played by indigenous communities in shaping the nation's governance system.

Bolivia, known as Hispanic America's poorest nation, has long struggled with political inequality and marginalization. However, in recent decades, the indigenous population has successfully mobilized to demand greater representation and recognition.

One of the most significant developments in Bolivia's political history was the rise and fall of Evo Morales and the Movement for Socialism (MAS) party. Morales, an indigenous Aymara, became the first indigenous president of Bolivia in 2006. His election marked a turning point in the country's history, as indigenous people, who make up a majority of the population, finally gained a voice in the highest office of the land.

Under Morales' leadership, Bolivia witnessed a series of transformative changes. The government implemented policies to alleviate poverty, address social inequality, and empower indigenous communities. These efforts included land redistribution, nationalization of natural resources, and the promotion of indigenous cultures and languages.

However, Morales' presidency also faced controversy and challenges. Accusations of political corruption and authoritarianism marred his tenure, leading to protests and eventual resignation in 2019. This event showcased the complexities and tensions inherent in Bolivia's political landscape.

The subchapter also explores the struggles of indigenous peoples against political corruption and governance issues. Despite their increased representation, indigenous communities continue to face obstacles in achieving full political equality. The fight against corruption and the establishment of transparent governance systems remain ongoing challenges for Bolivia.

Moreover, the impact of natural resource extraction on Bolivia's political economy cannot be ignored. The exploitation of resources such as gas, oil, and minerals has often resulted in environmental degradation and social unrest. Indigenous communities have been at the forefront of movements demanding more sustainable and equitable resource management.

The subchapter also delves into the influence of international organizations like the United Nations and World Bank on Bolivia's political history. These organizations have played a significant role in shaping policies related to poverty reduction, human rights, and sustainable development in the country.

Furthermore, the subchapter examines the role of women in Bolivian politics and their fight for gender equality. Women have been instrumental in advocating for social change and challenging patriarchal norms. Their participation in politics has been crucial in promoting inclusive governance and representation.

Lastly, the subchapter explores Bolivia's political relationships with neighboring countries in South America. The nation's geopolitical position and historical ties have shaped its foreign policy and regional alliances.

Understanding the indigenous representation in Bolivian politics is essential for diplomats and those interested in Bolivia's political history. It provides insights into the struggles, achievements, and ongoing challenges faced by indigenous communities in their quest for political equality and social justice.

Chapter 5: Bolivia's Struggles with Political Corruption and Governance

Historical Overview of Political Corruption in Bolivia

Political corruption has been a pervasive issue in Bolivia throughout its history, greatly impacting the country's governance and socio-economic development. Understanding the roots and evolution of this corruption is crucial for diplomats seeking to comprehend Bolivia's political history.

Bolivia's political corruption can be traced back to the colonial era, when the Spanish conquistadors exploited the country's rich natural resources for their own gain. This legacy of exploitation laid the foundation for a culture of corruption that continued to permeate Bolivia's political landscape even after gaining independence.

In the early years of independence, Bolivia's role in the Latin American independence movement was overshadowed by internal power struggles and rampant corruption. Political elites, often representing the interests of foreign powers, exploited Bolivia's resources and marginalized the indigenous majority.

The rise and fall of Evo Morales and the Movement for Socialism (MAS) party in Bolivia provides a significant case study of the country's struggle with political corruption. Morales, the first indigenous president, initially promised to fight corruption and empower marginalized groups. However, his prolonged stay in power led to allegations of abuse of power, nepotism, and embezzlement, which eroded public trust and ultimately led to his downfall.

Indigenous peoples have played a crucial role in shaping Bolivia's political landscape, advocating for their rights and challenging the corrupt political elites. Their struggles for representation and inclusion have had a significant impact on Bolivia's political history, leading to the recognition of indigenous rights and the rise of indigenous leaders in recent years.

Bolivia's struggles with political corruption and governance have been exacerbated by the country's heavy dependence on natural resource extraction. The exploitation of resources, particularly gas and minerals, has fueled corruption, as powerful elites have profited at the expense of the population and the environment.

International organizations such as the United Nations and World Bank have influenced Bolivia's political history by providing financial support and imposing conditions on governance and anti-corruption measures. Their involvement has both exacerbated and alleviated corruption, depending on the effectiveness of their interventions.

The role of women in Bolivian politics and their fight for gender equality is another important aspect of Bolivia's political history. Women have long been marginalized in political decision-making processes, but their activism and advocacy have led to significant advancements in gender equality and representation.

Bolivia's political relationship with its neighboring countries in South America has been shaped by historical rivalries, territorial disputes, and ideological differences. Understanding these dynamics is crucial for diplomats seeking to navigate Bolivia's regional alliances and conflicts.

Finally, the evolution of Bolivia's political parties and their ideologies throughout history provides insights into the changing dynamics of power and governance. From traditional political elites to the rise of grassroots movements, these ideological shifts have both fueled and challenged corruption in Bolivia.

In conclusion, Bolivia's historical overview of political corruption highlights the deep-rooted challenges the country has faced in its governance. Diplomats must understand this context to effectively engage with Bolivia and support efforts to combat corruption, strengthen democratic institutions, and promote inclusive governance.

High-Profile Corruption Scandals and their Impact on Governance

Corruption has been a persistent challenge in Bolivia's political history, leading to numerous high-profile scandals that have had a significant impact on the country's governance. This subchapter delves into these scandals, their consequences, and the lessons learned for diplomats seeking to understand Bolivia's political landscape.

Bolivia has witnessed several corruption scandals that have shaken the foundations of its governance. One of the most notorious cases was the "Bolivian Water War" in 2000, where the government's decision to privatize the water supply led to widespread protests and allegations of corruption. The scandal exposed the deep-rooted corruption within the political elite and fueled public discontent, eventually leading to the downfall of the government.

Another significant corruption scandal that rocked Bolivia was the "Petrobras scandal" in 2014, which implicated high-ranking officials, including the president at the time. This scandal revealed the extent of corruption within the country's energy sector, with millions of dollars being siphoned off through illicit practices. The fallout from this scandal severely undermined public trust in the government and further eroded Bolivia's governance structures.

These high-profile corruption scandals have had far-reaching consequences for Bolivia's governance. They have eroded public confidence in political institutions, weakened the rule of law, and hindered effective policy implementation. The scandals have also exacerbated social inequalities, as resources meant for public welfare have been diverted for personal gain.

To address these challenges, Bolivia has made efforts to combat corruption and strengthen governance. The establishment of specialized anti-corruption agencies and the enactment of stricter legislation have been important steps towards tackling corruption. Additionally, international organizations like the United Nations and World Bank have played a crucial role in supporting Bolivia's anti-corruption efforts and promoting good governance practices.

For diplomats, understanding the impact of corruption scandals on governance is vital for engaging with Bolivia effectively. It is important to comprehend the underlying causes and consequences of corruption, as well as the efforts made by the government to combat it. By engaging with local stakeholders, diplomats can support initiatives that promote transparency, accountability, and the rule of law.

In conclusion, high-profile corruption scandals have had a profound impact on Bolivia's governance. These scandals have eroded public trust, hindered effective policy implementation, and perpetuated social inequalities. However, Bolivia has taken steps to address corruption and strengthen governance structures. Diplomats can play a crucial role in supporting these efforts and promoting good governance practices in Bolivia.

Efforts to Combat Corruption and Improve Governance

Corruption and governance have been long-standing challenges in Bolivia, hindering the nation's progress and perpetuating poverty. However, in recent years, significant efforts have been made to combat corruption and improve governance, aiming to transform Bolivia into a more transparent and accountable nation.

One of the key initiatives in combating corruption has been the establishment of specialized anti-corruption agencies. These agencies, such as the Plurinational Special Force against Corruption (FEC) and the Control System for the Fight against Corruption (SISFC), have been created to investigate and prosecute corruption cases at all levels of government. Through their work, they have successfully exposed high-ranking officials involved in corrupt practices, leading to their prosecution and subsequent imprisonment.

Furthermore, Bolivia has also implemented legal reforms to strengthen its anti-corruption framework. The passing of the Anti-Corruption Law in 2010 provided the legal basis for the fight against corruption, establishing stricter penalties for corrupt individuals and fostering a culture of integrity in public administration. Additionally, the Whistleblower Protection Law was enacted to encourage individuals to report corruption without fear of retaliation, thus promoting a more transparent society.

In terms of governance, Bolivia has taken steps to enhance transparency and accountability in public administration. The creation of the Supreme Electoral Tribunal (TSE) has played a crucial role in ensuring free and fair elections, thereby promoting democratic governance. The TSE oversees the electoral process, guarantees the integrity of the electoral system, and safeguards citizens' right to vote.

Bolivia has also sought to strengthen its institutions and improve public service delivery. The implementation of the National Plan for Good Government has aimed to enhance the efficiency and effectiveness of public administration, ensuring that public resources are utilized for the benefit of all citizens. Moreover, the government has invested in capacity-building programs for public officials, equipping them with the necessary skills and knowledge to carry out their duties with integrity.

While significant progress has been made, challenges remain in the fight against corruption and the improvement of governance in Bolivia. Sustaining these efforts will require continued political will, allocation of resources, and the active participation of civil society. The international community, including organizations like the United Nations and the World Bank, can play a crucial role in supporting Bolivia's endeavors by providing technical assistance and financial support.

Ultimately, the fight against corruption and the improvement of governance are vital for Bolivia's sustainable development and its ability to address the needs of its citizens. By combating corruption and fostering transparency, Bolivia can build a stronger foundation for political stability, economic growth, and social progress.

Chapter 6: The Impact of Natural Resource Extraction on Bolivia's Political Economy

Bolivia's Abundance of Natural Resources

Bolivia, nestled in the heart of South America, is a country blessed with an abundance of natural resources. From vast mineral deposits to fertile agricultural lands, Bolivia's wealth in resources has defined its political history and shaped its position in the region. This subchapter explores the significance of Bolivia's natural resources and their impact on its political and economic landscape.

Minerals have played a pivotal role in Bolivia's history, with the country being one of the world's largest producers of silver, tin, and zinc. The discovery of these minerals during the colonial era attracted foreign powers, sparking conflicts and shaping Bolivia's political destiny. The exploitation of these resources fueled economic growth but also led to social inequalities and political unrest.

Furthermore, Bolivia boasts vast reserves of natural gas and oil, making it an important player in the global energy market. The extraction and export of these resources have influenced Bolivia's political economy, as the government has sought to strike a balance between maximizing revenues and ensuring the welfare of its citizens. The subchapter delves into the challenges faced by Bolivia in managing its natural resources sustainably and the impact of resource extraction on the environment and indigenous communities.

The international community has also played a significant role in Bolivia's natural resource sector. The United Nations and the World Bank have provided assistance and guidance in promoting sustainable development and ensuring responsible resource management. The subchapter explores the influence of these organizations on Bolivia's political history and their efforts to mitigate the negative impacts of resource extraction.

In addition to minerals and energy, Bolivia possesses vast agricultural lands and biodiversity. The subchapter sheds light on the role of agriculture in Bolivia's economy and the challenges faced by the country in achieving food security and sustainable agriculture practices.

Understanding Bolivia's abundance of natural resources is crucial for diplomats seeking to comprehend the complexities of the country's political history. By examining the interplay between resource wealth, governance, and social dynamics, diplomats can gain insights into Bolivia's past, present, and future. This subchapter provides a comprehensive overview of the impact of natural resources on Bolivia's political economy and offers a foundation for understanding the country's broader political history and challenges.

Historical Context of Resource Extraction in Bolivia

The historical context of resource extraction in Bolivia has played a significant role in shaping the country's political history. This subchapter aims to provide diplomats with a comprehensive understanding of how Bolivia's rich natural resources have influenced its political economy and governance.

Colonialism serves as the starting point for understanding the exploitation of Bolivia's resources. During the Spanish colonial rule, Bolivia's silver mines were a vital source of wealth for the Spanish Empire. The extraction of silver had profound consequences on Bolivia's political landscape, as it led to the rise of powerful mining elites and a stark social divide between the wealthy and the impoverished.

The impact of resource extraction continued long after independence, as Bolivia's natural resources remained a target for foreign exploitation.

The discovery of tin in the late 19th century brought about a new wave of foreign investment and increased extraction. This influx of wealth led to the rise of tin magnates and further exacerbated inequalities within Bolivian society.

The struggle for control over Bolivia's resources has been a recurring theme throughout its political history. The nationalization of Bolivia's oil and gas industry in the 1930s, led by President Hernando Siles, was an attempt to regain control over these valuable assets. However, subsequent governments faced challenges in managing and distributing the wealth generated by resource extraction, often leading to political instability and corruption.

The impact of natural resource extraction on Bolivia's political economy cannot be understated. The country's economic dependence on resource exports has created a vulnerable economy susceptible to fluctuations in global commodity prices. Additionally, the extraction industries have caused environmental degradation and contributed to social conflicts, particularly with indigenous communities who are often disproportionately affected by the negative consequences of resource extraction.

International organizations like the United Nations and World Bank have played a role in Bolivia's political history concerning resource extraction. These organizations have influenced policies related to resource management and sustainable development, aiming to mitigate the negative impacts of extraction and promote equitable distribution of wealth.

Understanding the historical context of resource extraction is crucial for diplomats engaging with Bolivia. It provides insight into the challenges the country faces in terms of governance, corruption, social inequality, and environmental sustainability. By comprehending the complexities of Bolivia's resource extraction history, diplomats can better navigate and engage with the country's political landscape, fostering diplomatic relations that address the needs and aspirations of Bolivia's diverse population.

Resource Nationalization and Economic Policies

Bolivia: A Diplomat's Guide to Understanding the Political History of Hispanic America's Poorest Nation

Resource nationalization and economic policies have played a significant role in shaping Bolivia's political history and its position as one of the poorest nations in Hispanic America. This subchapter explores the complexities of Bolivia's resource nationalization efforts and the impact of economic policies on the country's political landscape.

Bolivia, rich in natural resources such as natural gas, minerals, and oil, has long grappled with the challenge of maximizing the benefits of these resources for its people. Historically, Bolivia has experienced exploitation by foreign powers, leading to the rise of resource nationalism as a means to reclaim control over its resources. The nationalization of key industries, such as oil and gas, became a central pillar of Bolivia's economic policies.

Under the leadership of Evo Morales and the Movement for Socialism (MAS) party, Bolivia witnessed a period of increased resource nationalization. Morales championed the idea of "Bolivianization," aiming to ensure that the profits from resource extraction were reinvested into social programs and infrastructure development. However, the implementation of these policies was not without challenges, as they faced resistance from multinational corporations and internal political opposition.

The impact of natural resource extraction on Bolivia's political economy cannot be understated. While resource nationalization promised economic independence and social development, it also created a heavy reliance on commodity exports, leaving Bolivia vulnerable to fluctuations in global commodity prices. This overdependence on resource extraction has hindered the diversification of Bolivia's economy, perpetuating its status as one of the poorest nations in Hispanic America.

International organizations, such as the United Nations and World Bank, have played a role in Bolivia's political history. These organizations have provided financial support and guidance for economic reforms and development projects. However, their influence has also been met with criticism, as some argue that their policies have perpetuated dependency and failed to address the root causes of poverty and inequality in Bolivia.

Bolivia's struggle with political corruption and governance has further complicated the implementation of effective economic policies. Corruption scandals, mismanagement of resources, and a lack of transparency have eroded public trust and hindered Bolivia's progress towards economic stability.

Despite these challenges, Bolivia's political history also highlights the resilience and agency of its people. The role of indigenous peoples in shaping Bolivia's political landscape cannot be overlooked. Indigenous movements have emerged as powerful forces for change, advocating for the rights of marginalized communities and pushing for greater inclusion in political decision-making processes.

In conclusion, resource nationalization and economic policies have played a crucial role in Bolivia's political history and its position as one of Hispanic America's poorest nations. The country's struggle with political corruption, the impact of natural resource extraction, and the influence of international organizations have all shaped Bolivia's economic trajectory. However, the resilience of its people and the role of indigenous movements offer hope for a more inclusive and equitable political landscape in the future.

Environmental Concerns and Social Movements

Environmental concerns and social movements have played a crucial role in shaping Bolivia's political history. As a nation rich in natural resources, Bolivia has faced numerous challenges in balancing economic development with environmental sustainability. This subchapter explores the intricate relationship between environmental concerns and social movements in Bolivia, highlighting their impact on the country's political landscape.

Bolivia's political history has been deeply intertwined with its natural resources. The extraction of these resources often led to environmental degradation and social inequality, sparking widespread discontent among the population. Social movements emerged as a powerful force, advocating for the protection of the environment and the rights of indigenous communities.

One of the key environmental concerns in Bolivia is the deforestation of the Amazon rainforest. Activists and indigenous groups have mobilized to preserve this vital ecosystem, recognizing the importance of environmental preservation for future generations. These movements have successfully pushed for legislation and policies that aim to protect the Amazon and promote sustainable practices.

Moreover, the impact of climate change has further heightened environmental concerns in Bolivia. The country has experienced severe droughts, melting glaciers, and increased vulnerability to natural disasters. Social movements have called for urgent action to mitigate the effects of climate change and ensure the resilience of local communities.

The intersection of environmental concerns and social movements has also given rise to a broader movement for social justice in Bolivia. Indigenous peoples, who bear the brunt of environmental degradation, have fought for their rights and representation in the political sphere.

Their demands for land rights, cultural recognition, and equal opportunities have reshaped Bolivia's political landscape.

Furthermore, international organizations like the United Nations and the World Bank have played a significant role in addressing Bolivia's environmental concerns. These institutions have provided funding and technical assistance for sustainable development projects, influencing Bolivia's political decision-making process.

In conclusion, environmental concerns and social movements have become crucial drivers of change in Bolivia's political history. They have shed light on the need for sustainable development, social justice, and the preservation of natural resources. As diplomats, understanding the complex dynamics between environmental concerns, social movements, and politics is essential for navigating Bolivia's political landscape and fostering meaningful partnerships for a sustainable future.

Chapter 7: The Influence of International Organizations on Bolivia's Political History

The United Nations and its Role in Bolivian Politics

The United Nations (UN) has played a significant role in shaping Bolivian politics throughout its history. As a diplomatic body representing the collective interests of its member states, the UN has been actively involved in promoting peace, stability, and development in Bolivia.

One of the key contributions of the UN to Bolivian politics has been in the area of governance and democracy. The UN has supported Bolivia in its efforts to strengthen democratic institutions, promote respect for human rights, and ensure transparent and accountable governance. Through its various agencies and programs, the UN has provided technical assistance, capacity building, and policy advice to help Bolivia improve its democratic processes and institutions.

In addition, the UN has been instrumental in addressing social and economic challenges in Bolivia. The organization has supported the government's efforts to reduce poverty, improve healthcare and education, and promote sustainable development. Through its agencies, such as the United Nations Development Programme (UNDP) and the World Food Programme (WFP), the UN has implemented projects and programs aimed at improving the living conditions of the Bolivian people.

Furthermore, the UN has played a crucial role in resolving conflicts and promoting peace in Bolivia. It has supported dialogue and mediation processes to address political tensions and social unrest. The UN has also facilitated peacekeeping missions and provided humanitarian assistance in times of crisis, such as during natural disasters or political upheavals.

Moreover, the UN has been a platform for Bolivia to engage with the international community and voice its concerns on global issues. Through its participation in the UN General Assembly and other forums, Bolivia has been able to express its perspectives on matters such as climate change, indigenous rights, and social justice.

Overall, the United Nations has been a significant player in Bolivian politics, contributing to the country's democratic development, social progress, and international engagement. Its role in promoting peace, supporting governance, and addressing socio-economic challenges has been crucial in shaping Bolivia's political landscape. As diplomats, understanding the influence of the UN on Bolivia's political history is essential for comprehending the dynamics of this nation and its relationship with the international community.

The World Bank and its Impact on Bolivia's Economic Policies

The World Bank, an international financial institution, has played a significant role in shaping Bolivia's economic policies throughout its history. This subchapter will delve into the influence of the World Bank on Bolivia's political history, particularly focusing on its impact on the country's economic development.

Since its inception in 1944, the World Bank has been dedicated to providing financial and technical assistance to developing countries. Bolivia, being one of the poorest nations in Hispanic America, has been a recipient of substantial World Bank aid and loans over the years.

The World Bank's involvement in Bolivia's economic policies has been instrumental in several ways. Firstly, it has provided financial support for various development projects in the country, such as infrastructure development, education, healthcare, and poverty reduction initiatives.

These investments have aimed to improve the living conditions of Bolivians and foster economic growth.

Additionally, the World Bank has also influenced Bolivia's economic policies through its policy advice and conditionality. In exchange for financial assistance, the World Bank often requires recipient countries to implement specific economic reforms and policy adjustments. These conditions have sometimes been controversial, as they have pushed Bolivia to adopt neoliberal economic policies that have been criticized for their impact on vulnerable populations.

One example of the World Bank's influence on Bolivia is the structural adjustment programs implemented in the 1980s and 1990s. These programs aimed to liberalize and deregulate the Bolivian economy, privatize state-owned enterprises, and reduce public spending. While these measures were intended to promote economic growth and attract foreign investment, they also led to social unrest and increased inequality in the country.

However, it is essential to note that Bolivia's relationship with the World Bank has evolved over time. In recent years, the Bolivian government, led by the Movement for Socialism (MAS) party, has pursued a more independent economic path, distancing itself from the World Bank's influence. Under the leadership of President Evo Morales, Bolivia nationalized key industries, increased government control over natural resources, and redirected state revenues towards social programs.

In conclusion, the World Bank has had a significant impact on Bolivia's economic policies throughout its history. Its financial assistance and policy advice have shaped the country's development trajectory, sometimes with both positive and negative consequences. However, in recent years, Bolivia has sought to assert its economic independence and reduce its reliance on external institutions like the World Bank.

International Aid and Development Projects in Bolivia

Bolivia, known as Hispanic America's poorest nation, has long been the focus of international aid and development projects aimed at addressing its political, economic, and social challenges. This subchapter delves into the various initiatives undertaken by the international community to support Bolivia's development and shape its political history.

Since gaining independence from Spain in the early 19th century, Bolivia has faced numerous obstacles in its path towards progress. From the impact of colonialism to political corruption and governance struggles, the nation has grappled with a complex web of challenges. Recognizing the need for external assistance, international organizations like the United Nations and World Bank have played a significant role in Bolivia's political history.

These organizations have provided financial and technical support for a range of projects aimed at improving governance, reducing poverty, and promoting sustainable development. One such project was the establishment of microfinance programs, which aimed to empower marginalized communities and promote entrepreneurship. These initiatives have helped many Bolivians access credit and start their own businesses, contributing to economic growth and poverty reduction.

Additionally, international aid has been crucial in addressing Bolivia's struggles with political corruption. Through capacity-building programs, diplomats and experts have worked with local authorities to strengthen institutions, promote transparency, and ensure accountability. These efforts have helped Bolivia combat corruption and improve governance practices, paving the way for a more stable and prosperous future.

Furthermore, international aid has sought to address Bolivia's political relationship with its neighboring countries in South America. Diplomatic initiatives have focused on fostering dialogue, promoting regional integration, and resolving conflicts. By encouraging cooperation and understanding, these projects have contributed to a more peaceful and stable political landscape in Bolivia and the wider region.

Moreover, international aid has supported the role of indigenous peoples in shaping Bolivia's political landscape. Recognizing the importance of indigenous rights and representation, diplomats have worked closely with indigenous communities to promote their inclusion in decision-making processes. This has resulted in the rise of indigenous leaders in Bolivian politics, such as Evo Morales, who led the Movement for Socialism (MAS) party.

In conclusion, international aid and development projects have played a crucial role in Bolivia's political history. Through initiatives focused on governance, poverty reduction, regional cooperation, and indigenous rights, the international community has supported Bolivia's journey towards a more inclusive, stable, and prosperous nation. However, ongoing challenges persist, including the impact of natural resource extraction and the fight for gender equality. Diplomats and stakeholders must continue to collaborate and innovate to address these issues and shape Bolivia's political future.

Chapter 8: The Role of Women in Bolivian Politics and their Fight for Gender Equality

Gender Inequality in Bolivian Society

Gender inequality is a pervasive issue in Bolivian society, deeply rooted in its political history and social fabric. This subchapter explores the various aspects of gender inequality in Bolivia, shedding light on the challenges faced by women in the country and their fight for gender equality.

Bolivia, as the poorest nation in Hispanic America, has long struggled with gender disparities. Throughout its political history, women have been marginalized and excluded from positions of power and influence. Despite significant progress in recent years, gender inequality remains a pressing issue that demands attention.

The impact of colonialism on Bolivia's political history cannot be undermined in understanding the roots of gender inequality. The patriarchal systems introduced by the colonial powers perpetuated the subordination of women, relegating them to traditional roles within the family and society. These deeply ingrained norms continue to shape gender dynamics in Bolivia today.

The rise and fall of Evo Morales and the Movement for Socialism (MAS) party in Bolivia brought attention to the role of indigenous peoples in shaping the country's political landscape. While indigenous women played a crucial role in mobilizing support for Morales, they continue to face multiple layers of discrimination due to their gender and ethnicity.

Bolivia's struggles with political corruption and governance further exacerbate gender inequality. The unequal distribution of resources and power disproportionately affects women, limiting their access to education, healthcare, and economic opportunities. Moreover, the influence of natural resource extraction on Bolivia's political economy widens the gender gap, as women bear the brunt of environmental degradation and resource conflicts.

International organizations like the United Nations and World Bank have played a significant role in Bolivia's political history, attempting to address gender inequality through various initiatives. However, progress has been slow, and the challenges persist.

Despite these obstacles, women in Bolivia have been at the forefront of the fight for gender equality, actively participating in politics and advocating for their rights. Their resilience and determination have led to significant gains, including the adoption of gender quotas and the election of women to key positions in government.

In conclusion, gender inequality is a complex issue deeply intertwined with Bolivia's political history. While progress has been made, there is still much work to be done to achieve true gender equality in the country. Diplomats must understand the nuances of this issue and support initiatives that empower women and challenge the systemic barriers they face. By doing so, Bolivia can create a more inclusive and equitable society for all its citizens.

Women's Suffrage and Political Participation

In the subchapter titled "Women's Suffrage and Political Participation," we delve into the crucial role that women have played in Bolivia's political history. This chapter aims to shed light on the struggles faced by women in their fight for gender equality and their journey towards increased political participation.

Bolivia, like many countries, has a complex history when it comes to women's suffrage. It wasn't until 1952 that women were granted the right to vote in national elections. This landmark achievement was a result of the tireless efforts of women's rights activists who fought for their voices to be heard.

Throughout the years, women have continued to make significant strides in their political participation. Today, their influence can be seen across all levels of government, with women occupying key positions in legislative bodies, executive branches, and even the presidency. This progress is a testament to the determination and resilience of Bolivian women in their pursuit of equal rights and representation.

The fight for gender equality in Bolivia's political landscape has not been without challenges. Traditional gender roles and societal norms have posed obstacles for women seeking to enter politics. Additionally, women have faced discrimination and prejudice, further hindering their political aspirations. However, despite these barriers, women have persisted and forged a path towards greater inclusion and representation.

It is important to recognize the invaluable contributions made by women in shaping Bolivia's political history. Their unique perspectives and experiences have enriched the country's political discourse and policies. From championing social justice and human rights to advocating for environmental sustainability, women have played a vital role in addressing the pressing issues faced by Bolivia.

Moving forward, it is crucial for diplomats and policymakers to support and amplify the voices of women in Bolivian politics. By ensuring gender equality and creating an inclusive political environment, Bolivia can harness the full potential of its female population and achieve sustainable development and prosperity.

In conclusion, the subchapter on "Women's Suffrage and Political Participation" highlights the significant role of women in Bolivia's political history. It underscores the challenges they have overcome and the progress they have made in their fight for gender equality. By recognizing the contributions of women in politics, diplomats can foster a more inclusive and representative political landscape in Bolivia.

Women's Movements and Activism for Gender Equality

Throughout Bolivia's political history, women have played a crucial role in shaping the nation's progress towards gender equality. This subchapter explores the dynamic women's movements and activism that have emerged in Bolivia, highlighting their contributions to the fight for gender equality.

Bolivia's women's movements have been instrumental in challenging patriarchal norms and advocating for women's rights. These movements have worked tirelessly to address issues such as gender-based violence, reproductive rights, and economic empowerment. They have organized protests, demonstrations, and public campaigns to raise awareness and demand change.

One of the most significant milestones in Bolivia's women's movements was the adoption of a new constitution in 2009, which recognized gender equality as a fundamental principle. This constitutional reform was a result of the tireless efforts of women's organizations and activists who lobbied for the inclusion of gender-sensitive policies.

Moreover, women's movements have also been successful in increasing women's political representation. Bolivian women have made significant strides in breaking gender barriers in politics, with the election of the country's first indigenous woman president, Jeanine Áñez, in 2019. This achievement demonstrates the determination and resilience of Bolivian women in challenging the traditional power structures.

However, despite these advancements, challenges still persist. Gender-based violence and discrimination remain prevalent in Bolivian society. Women's movements continue to fight against these injustices, advocating for stronger laws and policies to protect women's rights and ensure their full participation in political and economic spheres.

Diplomats must understand the significance of women's movements and activism in Bolivia's political history. By recognizing the contributions and challenges faced by women, diplomats can actively support and promote gender equality in their diplomatic engagements. They can utilize their positions to advocate for policies that promote women's rights, engage with women's organizations, and support initiatives that empower women economically and politically.

Ultimately, the success of Bolivia's journey towards gender equality depends on the collective efforts of both Bolivian society and the international community. Diplomats have a crucial role to play in fostering dialogue, sharing best practices, and supporting initiatives that promote gender equality, ensuring a more inclusive and equitable future for Bolivia and its people.

Chapter 9: Bolivia's Political Relationship with its Neighboring Countries in South America

Historical Context of Bolivia's Relations with South American Nations

Bolivia's relations with South American nations have been shaped by a complex historical context that has influenced its political history. Understanding this context is crucial for diplomats seeking to navigate Bolivia's intricate web of regional alliances and conflicts.

Bolivia's role in the Latin American independence movement cannot be overstated. As one of the last countries to achieve independence from Spanish colonial rule, Bolivia's struggle for freedom resonated with other nations in the region. The legacy of this movement continues to shape Bolivia's relations with its South American counterparts. Diplomats must be aware of the shared history of liberation and the bonds of solidarity that exist between Bolivia and its neighbors.

The impact of colonialism on Bolivia's political history cannot be ignored. The exploitation of Bolivia's natural resources and the marginalization of its indigenous population have had lasting effects on the country's political landscape. Diplomats must be sensitive to these historical injustices and work towards promoting social justice and equality in their interactions with Bolivia.

The rise and fall of Evo Morales and the Movement for Socialism (MAS) party in Bolivia has had a profound impact on the country's relations with South American nations. Morales, Bolivia's first indigenous president, championed the rights of indigenous peoples and pursued a leftist agenda. His close ties with left-leaning governments in the region, such as Venezuela and Cuba, strained Bolivia's relations with more conservative nations. Diplomats must navigate these ideological divides and seek to build bridges between Bolivia and its neighbors.

The role of indigenous peoples in shaping Bolivia's political landscape cannot be underestimated. Bolivia has a large indigenous population that has long been marginalized and excluded from political power. Diplomats must be cognizant of the importance of indigenous rights and inclusion in their interactions with Bolivia, as well as in regional discussions on indigenous issues.

Bolivia's struggles with political corruption and governance have also had implications for its relations with South American nations. Diplomats must address these concerns and work towards promoting transparency and good governance in their engagements with Bolivia.

The impact of natural resource extraction on Bolivia's political economy is another key factor to consider. Bolivia is rich in natural resources, such as natural gas and minerals, which have both fueled economic growth and contributed to social and environmental challenges. Diplomats must be mindful of the complexities surrounding resource extraction and work towards promoting sustainable development and responsible resource management.

The influence of international organizations like the United Nations and World Bank on Bolivia's political history cannot be overlooked. Diplomats must be familiar with the role of these organizations in shaping Bolivia's development agenda and work towards aligning their efforts with Bolivia's national priorities.

The role of women in Bolivian politics and their fight for gender equality is another important aspect to consider. Bolivia has made significant progress in promoting gender equality, including enacting laws that promote women's political participation. Diplomats must support these efforts and work towards gender mainstreaming in their interactions with Bolivia.

Bolivia's political relationship with its neighboring countries in South America is characterized by both cooperation and conflict. Diplomats must be aware of the historical disputes and tensions that exist between Bolivia and its neighbors and work towards fostering dialogue and collaboration.

Finally, diplomats must understand the evolution of Bolivia's political parties and their ideologies throughout history. From conservative to leftist governments, Bolivia's political landscape has undergone significant transformations. Diplomats must be familiar with these shifts and adapt their strategies accordingly.

Overall, understanding the historical context of Bolivia's relations with South American nations is crucial for diplomats seeking to engage effectively with Bolivia and its neighbors. By considering these historical factors, diplomats can build stronger relationships, promote regional cooperation, and work towards a more prosperous and stable South America.

Border Disputes and Territorial Claims

One of the key aspects that have shaped Bolivia's political history is its border disputes and territorial claims. These conflicts have had a significant impact on the nation's relationships with neighboring countries and its overall political landscape. Understanding these disputes is essential for diplomats seeking to comprehend Bolivia's complex political history.

Bolivia has been involved in several territorial disputes throughout its existence. Perhaps the most notable is the ongoing conflict with Chile over access to the Pacific Ocean. The loss of its coastal territories during the War of the Pacific in the late 19th century has had lasting consequences for Bolivia's economic development and political stability. This dispute has remained a contentious issue, with Bolivia continuously seeking to regain access to the sea.

Another significant territorial claim involves Bolivia's dispute with Paraguay over the Chaco region. This dispute led to the devastating Chaco War between the two countries from 1932 to 1935, resulting in significant loss of life and resources. The outcome of this conflict further shaped Bolivia's geopolitical position and contributed to its political and economic challenges.

These border disputes and territorial claims have not only affected Bolivia's relations with neighboring countries but have also influenced its political parties and ideologies. Nationalistic sentiments and the desire to regain lost territories have been prominent themes in Bolivia's political discourse, shaping the ideologies of various political parties throughout history.

Furthermore, these disputes have also impacted Bolivia's relationship with international organizations such as the United Nations and the World Bank. Bolivia has sought international support in its territorial claims, often using these platforms to raise awareness and garner diplomatic backing. The influence of these organizations on Bolivia's political history cannot be understated, as they have played a role in mediating conflicts and shaping Bolivia's international standing.

In conclusion, border disputes and territorial claims have been integral to understanding Bolivia's political history. These conflicts have influenced the nation's relationships with neighboring countries, shaped its political parties and ideologies, and impacted its interactions with international organizations. For diplomats seeking to comprehend Bolivia's complex political landscape, an understanding of these disputes is crucial.

Economic and Political Cooperation Among South American Countries

In the realm of international diplomacy, fostering economic and political cooperation among nations is essential for mutual progress and stability. This is particularly true for South American countries, which share a common history and face similar challenges. Bolivia, as one of the poorest nations in Hispanic America, has played a pivotal role in shaping the economic and political landscape of the region. Understanding the dynamics of economic and political cooperation among South American countries is crucial for diplomats seeking to navigate Bolivia's political history.

South American countries have recognized the importance of collaboration and have formed various regional organizations to promote economic integration and political dialogue. The Union of South American Nations (UNASUR) and the Community of Latin American and Caribbean States (CELAC) are prime examples of these efforts. These organizations aim to enhance economic cooperation through the establishment of common markets, the facilitation of trade, and the promotion of investment among member countries. Additionally, they serve as platforms for political dialogue, allowing for the resolution of conflicts and the promotion of democratic values.

Bolivia has actively participated in these regional initiatives, recognizing the potential benefits of economic and political cooperation. The country has sought to strengthen its ties with neighboring nations, forging partnerships based on shared interests and common challenges. By collaborating with other South American countries, Bolivia has been able to leverage its resources and address pressing issues such as poverty, inequality, and environmental sustainability.

Furthermore, economic and political cooperation among South American countries has also been instrumental in shaping Bolivia's political history. The exchange of ideas and experiences has influenced the evolution of political parties and their ideologies throughout the nation's history. Additionally, regional cooperation has played a significant role in shaping Bolivia's relationship with international organizations such as the United Nations and the World Bank, providing opportunities for development assistance and foreign investment.

For diplomats engaged in Bolivia's political landscape, understanding the dynamics of economic and political cooperation among South American countries is crucial. It provides a broader context for comprehending Bolivia's political history, the struggles with corruption and governance, and the challenges faced by indigenous peoples and women in Bolivian politics. By recognizing the interconnectedness of South American nations and the potential for collaboration, diplomats can foster stronger relationships and contribute to the progress and stability of the region as a whole.

Chapter 10: The Evolution of Bolivia's Political Parties and their Ideologies Throughout History

Overview of Political Parties in Bolivia

Bolivia's political landscape has been shaped by a multitude of political parties that have emerged throughout its history. This subchapter provides a comprehensive overview of the various political parties in Bolivia, their ideologies, and their impact on the nation's political history.

Since the country's independence from Spain in 1825, Bolivia has witnessed the rise and fall of numerous political parties. These parties have represented a wide range of ideologies, including conservatism, liberalism, socialism, and indigenous rights.

One of the most influential parties in Bolivia's political history is the Movement for Socialism (MAS) party, led by Evo Morales. The MAS party, which was founded in 1997, gained significant popularity among the indigenous population and marginalized communities. Under Morales' leadership, the MAS party implemented various social and economic reforms, aimed at reducing poverty and inequality. However, Morales' long tenure as president also saw accusations of authoritarianism and corruption.

Indigenous peoples have played a crucial role in shaping Bolivia's political landscape. The emergence of indigenous-led parties, such as the MAS party, has brought attention to the rights and representation of indigenous communities in the country's political system. These parties have advocated for greater recognition and autonomy for indigenous peoples, challenging the traditional power structures dominated by the elite.

Bolivia has faced significant challenges with political corruption and governance. Several parties have been plagued by allegations of corruption and mismanagement, leading to a loss of public trust. Efforts to combat corruption and improve governance have been ongoing, with varying degrees of success.

The extraction and exploitation of Bolivia's natural resources have had a profound impact on its political economy. The control and distribution of wealth derived from these resources have been central issues in political debates and have influenced the ideologies of different parties throughout history.

Bolivia's political history has also been influenced by international organizations such as the United Nations and the World Bank. These organizations have provided financial assistance and influenced policy decisions, sometimes leading to tensions between the Bolivian government and international actors.

Women's participation in Bolivian politics and their fight for gender equality have gained momentum in recent years. Women's rights organizations and feminist movements have been instrumental in pushing for greater representation and opportunities for women in political decision-making processes.

Furthermore, Bolivia's political relationship with its neighboring countries in South America has been significant. The nation has been actively involved in regional integration initiatives and has sought to strengthen diplomatic ties with its neighbors.

In conclusion, Bolivia's political parties have played a crucial role in shaping the country's political history. The ideologies, actions, and impact of these parties have influenced Bolivia's struggle with corruption, governance, indigenous rights, gender equality, and its relationship with neighboring countries. Understanding the evolution of these parties is essential for diplomats and those interested in Bolivia's political history.

Historical Context of Party Formation and Ideological Shifts

The historical context of party formation and ideological shifts in Bolivia is a crucial aspect to understand the political history of this impoverished nation. Throughout the years, Bolivia has experienced numerous political changes, which have shaped its landscape and influenced its relations with neighboring countries in South America.

Bolivia's role in the Latin American independence movement cannot be understated. The country played a significant role in the fight for independence from Spain, with revolutionary leaders like Simon Bolivar and Antonio Jose de Sucre leading the charge. The struggle for independence laid the foundation for Bolivia's political history, setting the stage for the formation of political parties and the subsequent ideological shifts.

The impact of colonialism on Bolivia's political history has been profound. As one of the last colonies to gain independence, Bolivia faced the legacy of colonial rule, which left deep scars on its society. The remnants of colonialism, including the socio-economic disparities and racial inequalities, have influenced Bolivia's political landscape and the formation of political parties.

One of the most notable political figures in Bolivia's recent history is Evo Morales and his Movement for Socialism (MAS) party. Morales, the first indigenous president of Bolivia, rose to power on the platform of social justice and championing the rights of indigenous peoples. However, his presidency also witnessed controversies surrounding political corruption and governance, leading to his eventual fall from power.

The role of indigenous peoples in shaping Bolivia's political landscape cannot be ignored. Indigenous communities have long fought for their rights and representation in the political arena, leading to the emergence of indigenous-led political parties and movements.

Bolivia's struggles with political corruption and governance have been a persistent issue throughout its history. The country has grappled with corruption scandals and the challenge of establishing effective governance structures. These challenges have had significant ramifications on Bolivia's political parties and their ideologies.

The impact of natural resource extraction on Bolivia's political economy has been another key aspect of its political history. The exploitation of Bolivia's rich natural resources, such as gas and minerals, has influenced the country's economic policies and shaped the political discourse.

International organizations like the United Nations and World Bank have also played a role in Bolivia's political history. Their influence has impacted various aspects, including economic policies, social programs, and governance reforms.

The role of women in Bolivian politics and their fight for gender equality is a notable aspect of Bolivia's political history. Women have been actively involved in politics, advocating for their rights and pushing for gender equality in the political sphere.

Bolivia's political relationship with its neighboring countries in South America has been a dynamic and ever-evolving aspect. The country has navigated its relationships with countries like Brazil, Argentina, and Chile, facing geopolitical challenges and forging alliances.

Finally, the evolution of Bolivia's political parties and their ideologies throughout history has been a reflection of the changing social, economic, and political landscape. From conservative and liberal parties to the emergence of indigenous-led movements, Bolivia's political parties have adapted to the changing aspirations and demands of its people.

Understanding the historical context of party formation and ideological shifts in Bolivia is crucial for diplomats and those interested in Bolivia's political history. By delving into these topics, one can gain a comprehensive understanding of the factors that have shaped Bolivia's political landscape and its relations with neighboring countries.

Major Political Parties and their Platforms

Throughout its history, Bolivia has witnessed the rise and fall of various political parties, each with its own distinct platform and ideology. Understanding these parties and their platforms is crucial for diplomats seeking to navigate Bolivia's complex political landscape. This subchapter delves into the major political parties that have shaped Bolivia's history and their respective platforms.

One of the most influential parties in Bolivia's political history is the Movement for Socialism (MAS) party, led by Evo Morales. The MAS advocated for the rights and empowerment of Bolivia's indigenous population, who have historically been marginalized. Their platform encompassed land reform, nationalization of key industries, and greater social inclusion. Under Morales' leadership, the MAS implemented various progressive policies that aimed to reduce poverty and inequality in the country.

However, Bolivia's political history is not solely defined by the MAS. Other major parties have also played significant roles. The Democratic Unity Coalition (UD) is a center-right party that emphasizes free-market policies, privatization, and fiscal discipline. They advocate for a smaller state and promote business-friendly policies to attract foreign investment.

Another important party is the Revolutionary Nationalist Movement (MNR), which emerged in the 1940s. The MNR sought to modernize Bolivia and reduce the influence of foreign powers. Their platform included nationalization of key industries, agrarian reform, and the promotion of indigenous rights.

Over the years, Bolivia has also witnessed the rise of various regional and indigenous parties, such as the Movement Without Fear (MSM) and the Pachakuti Indigenous Movement (MIP). These parties focus on regional autonomy, cultural preservation, and social justice for indigenous communities.

It is worth noting that Bolivia's political parties have evolved and adapted their platforms over time. External factors, such as the influence of international organizations like the United Nations and World Bank, have also shaped Bolivia's political history. Moreover, women in Bolivia have been fighting for gender equality and representation in politics, leading to the emergence of feminist parties and the inclusion of gender-related issues in party platforms.

By understanding the major political parties and their platforms, diplomats can gain valuable insights into Bolivia's political landscape. This knowledge enables them to engage with key stakeholders and contribute to the development of meaningful diplomatic relationships.

Conclusion: Understanding Bolivia's Political History and its Significance for Diplomats

In conclusion, understanding Bolivia's political history is of paramount importance for diplomats who wish to navigate the intricacies of Hispanic America's poorest nation. This subchapter has delved into various aspects that have shaped Bolivia's political landscape, providing valuable insights for diplomats seeking to engage with the country.

Bolivia's role in the Latin American independence movement cannot be understated. As a key player in the fight for liberation from Spanish colonial rule, Bolivia's history is intertwined with the broader struggle for independence in the region. Diplomats must grasp the significance of this legacy in order to comprehend Bolivia's political aspirations and national identity.

The impact of colonialism on Bolivia's political history has left a lasting imprint on the country. Diplomats need to understand the deep-rooted social, economic, and cultural consequences of colonial rule, which have shaped Bolivia's political trajectory. Recognizing the historical injustices endured by indigenous peoples is crucial for diplomats engaging with Bolivia's political landscape.

The rise and fall of Evo Morales and the Movement for Socialism (MAS) party in Bolivia demonstrates the complex dynamics of power and governance in the country. Diplomats must grasp the implications of Morales' presidency and the subsequent political changes that have followed. Understanding the aspirations and concerns of the indigenous communities that Morales represented is essential for effective diplomatic engagement.

Bolivia's struggles with political corruption and governance pose significant challenges for diplomats. The country's history is riddled with instances of corruption and poor governance, which have hindered its development and perpetuated social inequality. Diplomats must be aware of these issues and work towards promoting transparency and good governance in their interactions with Bolivia.

The impact of natural resource extraction on Bolivia's political economy cannot be ignored. Diplomats must comprehend the complex relationship between resource extraction, economic development, and political stability in Bolivia. Recognizing the environmental and social consequences of resource exploitation is crucial for sustainable diplomatic engagement.

International organizations like the United Nations and World Bank have played a significant role in Bolivia's political history. Diplomats must be aware of the influence exerted by these institutions and work towards promoting mutually beneficial partnerships that prioritize Bolivia's interests and development goals.

The role of women in Bolivian politics and their fight for gender equality is an important aspect of Bolivia's political history. Diplomats must acknowledge and support the efforts of women in politics, advocating for gender equality and empowering women to take on leadership roles in the country.

Bolivia's political relationship with its neighboring countries in South America is an essential dimension for diplomats to understand. Regional dynamics and alliances can significantly impact Bolivia's political landscape, and diplomats must navigate these relationships with sensitivity and strategic acumen.

The evolution of Bolivia's political parties and their ideologies throughout history provides crucial context for diplomats. Understanding the different political ideologies and their implications is vital for effective communication and collaboration with Bolivian political actors.

In conclusion, diplomats must immerse themselves in Bolivia's political history to comprehend the complexities and nuances of the country's political landscape. By understanding Bolivia's historical struggles, aspirations, and contemporary challenges, diplomats can forge meaningful connections and work towards mutually beneficial partnerships with this vibrant nation.